Explore Space!

Christa McAuliffe

by Thomas Streissguth

Consultant:
James Gerard
Aerospace Education Specialist
NASA Aerospace Education Services Program

Bridgestone Books
an imprint of Capstone Press
Mankato, Minnesota

Bridgestone Books are published by Capstone Press
151 Good Counsel Drive, P.O. Box 669, Mankato, Minnesota 56002
http://www.capstone-press.com

Library of Congress Cataloging-in-Publication Data
Streissguth, Thomas, 1958–
    Christa McAuliffe / by Thomas Streissguth.
        p. cm.—(Explore space!)
        Summary: Presents a brief biography of the school teacher who joined NASA's Teacher
in Space program and tragically died in the space shuttle Challenger disaster.
        Includes bibliographical references and index.
        ISBN 0-7368-1624-0 (hardcover)
        1. McAuliffe, Christa, 1948–1986—Juvenile literature. 2. Astronauts—United States—
Biography—Juvenile literature. 3. Teachers—New Hampshire—Biography—Juvenile
literature. 4. Challenger (Spacecraft)—Accidents—Juvenile literature. [1. McAuliffe, Christa,
1948–1986. 2. Astronauts. 3. Teachers. 4. Challenger (Spacecraft)—Accidents. 5. Women—
Biography.] I. Title. II. Series.
TL789.85.M33 S77 2003
629.45'0092—dc21   2002010138

Editorial Credits
Chris Harbo and Roberta Schmidt, editors; Karen Risch, product planning editor;
    Steve Christensen, series designer; Juliette Peters, cover and interior designer;
    Alta Schaffer, photo researcher

Photo Credits
Corbis, 10 (right); Bettmann, 16; Ross Pictures, 20
Corrigan Family, 6, 8 (both)
NASA, cover, 4, 10 (left), 12, 14, 18 (both)
PhotoDisc, 8 (background), 10 (background)

1 2 3 4 5 6 08 07 06 05 04 03

B
cAuliffe

HEM - 6766

Table of Contents

Christa McAuliffe

Christa McAuliffe was the first teacher to fly on a space mission. She joined six astronauts on board the space shuttle *Challenger*. This shuttle lifted off on January 28, 1986. *Challenger's* flight ended when the spacecraft exploded. The accident killed everyone on board.

space shuttle

a spacecraft that can fly into space and return to Earth many times

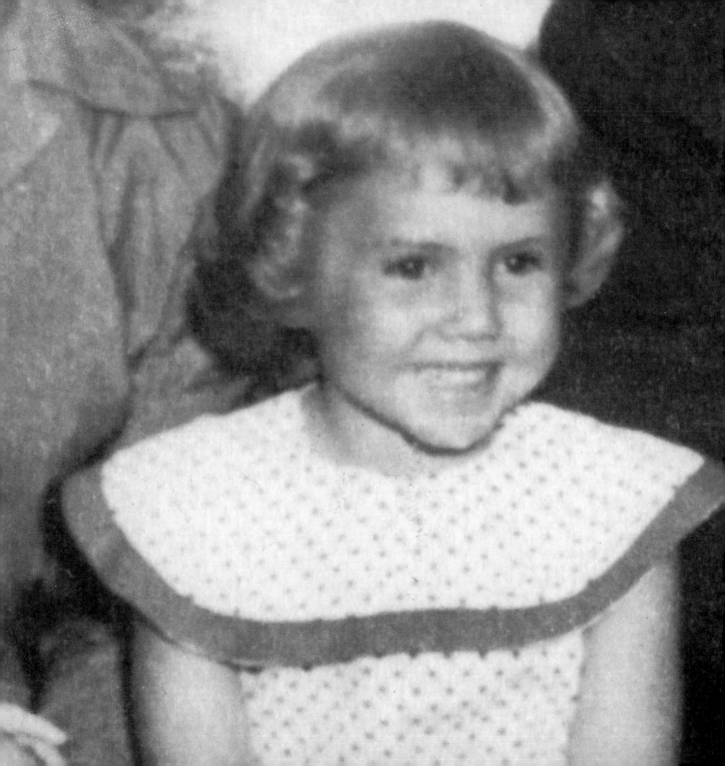

Christa's Early Years

Christa was born Sharon Christa Corrigan September 2, 1948. Her parents, Grace and Edward Corrigan, always called her Christa. Christa grew up in Framingham, Massachusetts. In high school, Christa played basketball and softball.

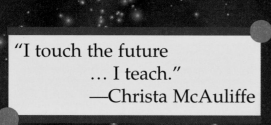

"I touch the future
... I teach."
—Christa McAuliffe

High School Teacher

In 1970, Christa earned an education degree from Framingham State College. That year, she married Steve McAuliffe. They moved to Washington, D.C. Christa became a high school history and social studies teacher. Steve studied law. By 1978, Christa and Steve had two children.

Teacher in Space Project

NASA

NASA believed a teacher could get students excited about space travel.

Teacher in Space Program

In 1984, Christa heard about NASA's Teacher in Space program. More than 11,000 teachers applied for the program. They had to describe a project they would do in space. Christa planned to write a diary during her mission. NASA chose Christa and nine other finalists for the program.

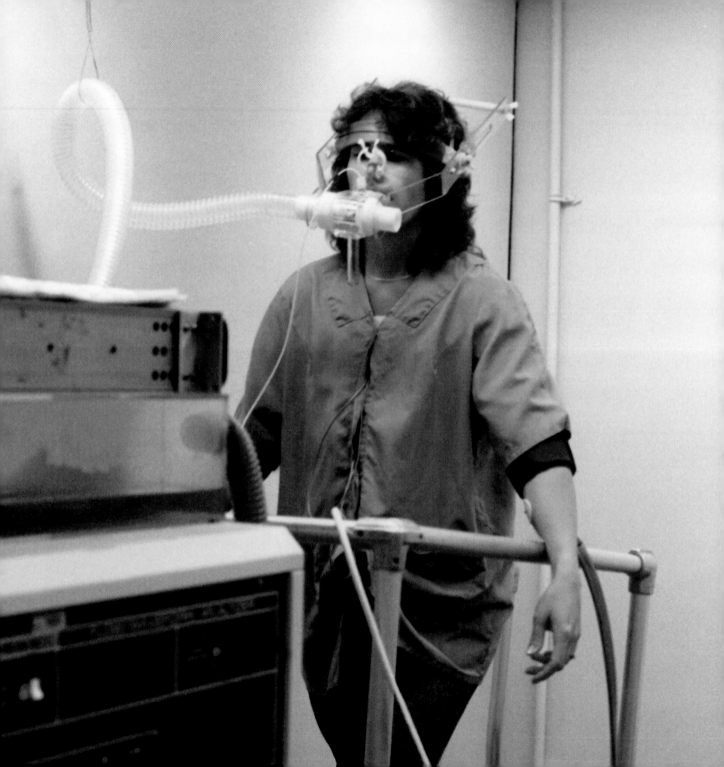

Medical Tests

The Teacher in Space finalists took many medical tests. Doctors checked Christa's heartbeat and blood pressure. They also checked her lungs and breathing. Christa had to run on a treadmill to test her muscles. She passed all of the tests.

blood pressure
a measure of how well the heart and arteries are pumping blood through the body

Space Training

In July 1985, NASA picked Christa to fly in the space shuttle *Challenger*. Christa trained for six months. She learned how to use computers and video cameras. She flew in NASA's KC-135 aircraft. This plane helped her get ready to be weightless in space.

weightless
free of the pull of gravity

15

Christa's parents, Edward and Grace Corrigan, talked to the media before *Challenger's* flight.

Support for Christa

Friends, family, and students all supported Christa. They wanted her to go on the spaceflight. NASA scientists helped Christa prepare science lessons to teach from space. The six other crew members helped Christa learn about the space shuttle.

The *Challenger* crew: back row (from left): Ellison S. Onizuka, Christa McAuliffe, Gregory B. Jarvis, Judith A. Resnik; front row (from left): Michael J. Smith, Francis R. Scobee, Ronald E. McNair

The Tragic Flight

Cold weather delayed the spaceflight. Finally, NASA ordered *Challenger* to fly on January 28, 1986. The cold weather damaged part of the spacecraft. *Challenger* exploded 73 seconds after liftoff. Christa and the other six astronauts died in the explosion.

delay
to stop for awhile

Remembering Christa

In 1987, a *Challenger* memorial was built in Arlington National Cemetery. The memorial shows the faces of the seven *Challenger* astronauts. In 1990, the Christa McAuliffe Planetarium opened in New Hampshire. The planetarium teaches students about outer space.

planetarium
a theater that shows the positions of the stars and planets on a curved ceiling

Important Dates

1948—Sharon Christa Corrigan is born September 2.

1970—Christa graduates from Framingham State College; she marries Steve McAuliffe on August 23; they move to Washington, D.C.

1978—Christa earns a master's degree in education from Bowie State College and moves to Concord, New Hampshire.

1982—Christa begins teaching at Concord High School.

1984—Christa McAuliffe applies for NASA's Teacher in Space program.

1985—NASA picks Christa to fly in the space shuttle *Challenger*.

1986—*Challenger* explodes 73 seconds after liftoff on January 28.

1990—The Christa McAuliffe Planetarium opens in Concord, New Hampshire.

Words to Know

astronaut (ASS-truh-nawt)—someone trained to fly into space in a spacecraft

diary (DYE-uh-ree)—a blank book in which people write down things that happened to them each day

graduate (GRAJ-oo-ate)—to finish all required classes at a school

gravity (GRAV-uh-tee)—a force that pulls objects together; gravity pulls objects down toward the center of Earth.

mission (MISH-uhn)—a planned job or task

space shuttle (SPAYSS SHUHT-uhl)—a spacecraft that can fly into space and return to Earth many times

weightless (WATE-liss)—free of the pull of gravity

Read More

Bredeson, Carmen. *The Challenger Disaster: Tragic Space Flight.* American Disasters. Berkeley Heights, N.J.: Enslow, 1999.

Jeffrey, Laura S. *Christa McAuliffe: A Space Biography.* Countdown to Space. Springfield, N.J.: Enslow, 1998.

Internet Sites

Track down many sites about Christa McAuliffe.
Visit the FACT HOUND at
http://www.facthound.com

IT IS EASY! IT IS FUN!

1) Go to *http://www.facthound.com*
2) Type in: 0736816240
3) Click on "FETCH IT" and FACT HOUND will find several links hand-picked by our editors.

Relax and let our pal FACT HOUND do the research for you!

Index